BEAUTIES OF ISLAM

*

BEAUTIES OF ISLAM

*

ANNIE BESANT

THE THEOSOPHICAL PUBLISHING HOUSE
Adyar, Chennai 600 020, India • Wheaton, IL, USA

© The Theosophical
Publishing House, Adyar

Seventh Reprint 2002

ISBN 81-7059-143-0

Printed at the Vasanta Press
The Theosophical Society
Adyar, Chennai 600 020, India

BEAUTIES OF ISLAM

AN EXPLANATION

I AM to speak this evening on Islam in the light of Theosophy. Let me begin by saying a word or two as to the relation of that which is called " Theosophy " to the great religions of the world. As you can at once see by the name, if we translate it into English, it means simply " Divine Wisdom ".

3

By that name is indicated THE
WISDOM in its relation to all the
religions of the world. Every religion in its turn has grown up
from the great Root of the Divine
Wisdom. Every religion in its place
is an exposition of the Divine Life
in humanity, and so this teaching
which takes only the name of the
Divine Wisdom, without any sec-
tarian limitation, is the fervent
helper and defender of every religion which has uplifted and con-
soled humanity. It is no one religion, but *every* religion, that has in
it a friend and a defender.

4

Sometimes some of our Christian brethren have regarded Theosophy as inimical to the great religion of the West. But that is a misconception, probably arising from the fact that Theosophy has strengthened eastern faith against aggression, and has also pointed out the additions and omissions which have injured popular Christianity in the present, just as it has pointed out similar additions and omissions in popular Hinduism and Buddhism. Theosophy has stood as a defender of every faith of the western or the eastern world. For everywhere in these days religion is attacked, and its defence becomes the duty of a true Theosophist; and in the East, especially in India, where the religions of Hinduism and Islam have their home and their numerous adherents, wherever those religions are attacked, Theosophy becomes defensive and stands in the breach against attacks, to explain, to illuminate and to defend. But none the less in the western lands, in Christendom, Theosophy is the servant of Christianity, as it is here the servant of Hinduism, Zoroastrianism and Islam. There, in the West, at last it is being recognised as filling up a great gap in the defence of Christianity, not against the attacks of any other religion but against the attacks of Materialism, against the attacks of scientific thought, where that scientific thought has no spiritual ideal. So everywhere Theosophy comes forward to explain and to illuminate.

———

In this country of India, where so large a proportion of Indians

belong to the great faith of the
Prophet Muhammad, there are
some seventy million people who
regard Him as the chief messenger
of God. Here naturally Theosophy comes in to help all those who
follow that faith. Their position
among the religions of the world is
not as fully recognised as it ought
to be; that is, Islam is not regarded
as it should be by very many, as
one of the great exponents of
Divine Wisdom. Taken as a religion, it is often unfairly attacked
because it is utterly misunderstood
as to the greatness of its Prophet

and the nobility of his teachings to the world. Oftentimes in the West you find attacks on Islam made on the ground that it is fanatically persecuting and not progressive; on the ground that the position of woman in Islam is not such as it should be; on the ground that it does not encourage learning, science and intellectual endeavour. These are the three chief attacks which the Westerns make against Islam. I want, towards the conclusion of what I have to say, to show you that these attacks are not justified by the teachings of the

Prophet, and are controverted by the services which Islam has rendered to the world. It is true that to-day Islam does not stand before the world as the exponent of high learning, of great intellectual endeavours, but that is not due to the fault of the teachings but rather to the neglecting of them. Islam has suffered, as all the other religions of the world have suffered, because its followers are unworthy of its Founder.

Now Islam differs from the other religions of the world in one important fact. With regard to its

Founder, the Prophet, there is no intermixture in his history of the mythic element which surrounds the other great religious Teachers; his life was led in times that are regarded as historical. In the seventh century of the Christian era, this man was born and lived out his life in lands the history of which is known.

How splendidly his life can face the light, how utterly ignorant are they who attack the Prophet Muhammad, is shown by history. Many do not know the history of his life—so simple, so heroic and so noble in its outlines; one of the great lives of historic men. He was born in difficult times, surrounded by difficult circumstances; born amongst a people who were sunk in superstition; born amidst a people in whom superstitions were bearing their most evil fruits. We shall see in a moment from the testimony of those he converted, from the words of those who bore witness to him whilst still he lived, and who held him Prophet of God, what were the lives of the masses of the people. But even before this, he stands out as a Light in the darkness, and we find his life so noble and so true that we realise why he was chosen out to bear to all those around him the Message of his Lord. What was the name by which all men, women, and children in Mecca knew him? It was the name of Al-Amin, the Trustworthy. I know of no higher and nobler epithet than that with which they named this man who had been amongst them from his youth—the man worthy of trust. It is told of him that when he walked in the streets, the children ran out from the doors and clung to his knees and hands. Where you have these two qualities in one character—the love of children and a character that makes the men around him call him the Trust-worthy—you have the elements of a hero, of a born Leader, of a Teacher of men.

It is a story of great significance, that of those fifteen weary years of struggle, of thoughts, of meditation, of living in the life of the world and then away for a time in the cave of the desert, he wrestled with thoughts that at first over-powered him, and he shrank with the weakness of a man against the call from the powers of Spirit. It is noteworthy that when he came back from that cave one night when the Angel of the Lord had bidden him: "Rise, O Prophet of God, and go forth and cry to the people," he shivered, fearing and doubting: "Who am I, what am I, that I should go as Prophet of the Lord?" It was then that his wife cheered him up, bidding him obey the call. "Fear not," she said, " art thou not the Trustworthy? Never will God deceive a man trusted by men." Nowhere can there be a fairer testimony to a Prophet. Then he went forth to his great mission, the wife of his bosom was his first disciple, that dearest and noblest of women who lived with this leader of men for twenty-six years of perfect married life. Such was the character of the man as judged by her who knew him best.

Now it is said popularly that a Prophet is without honour in his own country. This Prophet was not without honour in his own country and in his father's house. He was honoured in the hearts of

16

his relatives, and from them he won his first disciples. His wife, as just said, was his first disciple, and then came those who were nearest akin to him, and then others amongst those whom he loved. After three years of patient labour there were thirty who recognised him as the Prophet of the Lord. And how simple and frugal his life! He mended his broken shoes, patched his own coat—tailor and cobbler for himself, even when, towards the close of his life, thousands around him bowed down to him as Prophet. Such was

17

the character of the man—so simple, so noble, so straightforward.

One day he was talking to a rich man when a blind man cried aloud: " O Prophet of God, teach me the way of salvation." Muhammad did not listen, for he was talking to a wealthy man. Again he cried aloud: " O Prophet of God, show me the way of salvation." The Prophet frowned, and turned aside. On the very next morning there came a message that for ever remains in *Al Quran*, as testimony to his honesty and humility,

" wherein he put it that all might remember."

The Prophet frowned and turned aside because the blind man came to him; and how dost thou know whether he shall peradventure be cleansed from his sins, or whether he shall be admonished and the admonition shall profit him? The man who is wealthy thou receivest respectfully; whereas it is not to be charged on thee that he is not cleansed: but him who cometh unto thee earnestly seeking his salvation, and who feareth God, dost thou reject. By no means shouldst thou act thus.

Few men would be brave enough to publish such a reprimand, addressed directly to themselves; but, on the contrary, so great was this man and so true, that afterwards whenever he saw this blind man, he rose and brought him forward, saying: " Welcome, because it was for thee my Lord reprimanded me." So great he was that the slightest weakness and breach of kindness were promptly recognised, and the man who was the cause of the reprimand he held as dear and honoured him. No wonder that we find that all men loved him who were near to him.

This love that his immediate followers,who knew him personally, had for Muhammad was one of the most touching in the history of the world's religions. His followers were persecuted in a most ghastly way; they put them on the heated sand with the scorching Arabian sun burning down on them; they piled stones upon them; they refused them a single drop of water to moisten their parched lips; they tore them into fragments; one man was cut to pieces bit by bit, his flesh torn piecemeal from his bones, and they said to him in the midst of his agony: " Thou believest in thy Prophet; wouldst not thou rather that Muhammad were in thy place, and thou at home?" Answers the dying man: " As God is my witness, I would not be at home with wife and children and substance, if Muhammad were for that to be pricked by a single thorn." Thus you may learn how this man was loved by his followers.

There is nothing more pathetic than an incident which took place after a battle, one of the early battles where his troops had conquered, and there was great spoil taken. The Prophet divided the spoil, and those who were nearest to him and who had helped him longest and best had no share in the division. They were angered and secretly murmured. Thereat he called them around him and said:

"I have known a discourse you held among yourselves. When I came amongst you, you were wandering in darkness, and the Lord gave you the right direction; you were suffering, and He made you happy; at enmity among yourselves, and He has filled your hearts with brotherly love, and has given you victory. Was it not so, tell me?" "Indeed, it is even as thou sayest," was the reply; "to the Lord and His Prophet belong benevolence and grace." "Nay, by the Lord," continued the Prophet, "but ye might have answered, and answered truly—for I would have testified to its truth myself—'Thou camest to us rejected as an impostor and we believed in thee; thou camest as a helpless fugitive, and we assisted thee; poor and an outcast, and we gave thee an asylum; comfortless, and we solaced thee.' Why disturb your hearts because of the things of this life? Are ye not satified that others should obtain the flocks and the camels, while ye go back to your homes with me in your midst?"

And it is said that at these words from his lips, "tears ran down upon their beards," and they said: "Yea, Prophet of God, we are well satisfied with our share."

So much, then, he was loved; why? because he brought the Light to those who were in the darkness of ignorance. The testimony of his followers to what they were, and to what they had become by the teachings of the Prophet, stands on record; we can understand what they thought of him as Prophet, when the divine flash struck them by the teaching that he gave. They said in a petition still preserved:

We adored idols; we lived in unchastity; we ate dead bodies, and spoke abominations; we disregarded every feeling of humanity, and the duties of hospitality and neighbourhood; we knew no law but that of the strong; when God raised among us a Man, of whose birth, truthfulness, honesty and purity, we were aware; and he called us to the unity of God; and taught us not to associate anything with him, he forbade us the worship of idols, and enjoined us to speak the truth, to be faithful to our trusts, to be merciful, and to regard the rights of our neighbours; he forbade us to speak evil of women, or to devour the substance of orphans; he ordered us to fly from vices, and to abstain from evil, to offer prayers, to render alms, to observe the fast. We have believed in him, we have accepted his teachings.

Once he had some converts from whom he took a pledge, the pledge

of Akaba. As regards this pledge,
remember that you are not dealing
with a far-off time with no histor-
ians living, but you are dealing
with the time of the seventh century, when records were well kept.
See the pledge taken by these
followers of the Prophet:

We will not associate anything with
God; we will not steal, nor commit adul-
tery, nor fornication; we will not kill our
children; we will abstain from calumnies
and slander; we will obey the Prophet in
everything that is right; and we will be
faithful to him in weal and sorrow.

Such is the pledge. The very
words of the pledge speak eloquently

of the condition of the people whom he raised. Judge it by those things from which they promised to abstain. Human sacrifice was common, profligacy was widespread in ordinary life. Such was the pledge that he accepted, such was the promise that he took from his followers. See how wisely adapted to the needs of the time were his moral teachings.

I leave aside till later on, as I said, the question regarding women; the question regarding toleration, I will also deal with later on. But I want to show you here that he laid among the ignorant of his own people the firm foundation of a noble ethic. Take his teaching on charity, and see how he defined it. What is charity? One would say, giving alms, giving money to the poor. Nay, every good act is charity:

Your smiling in your brothers' face is charity; an exhortation addressed to your fellow-men to do virtuous deeds is equal to almsgiving. Putting a wanderer in the right path is charity; assisting the blind is charity; removing stones and thorns and other obstructions from the road is charity; giving water to the thirsty is charity.

So practical, so simple, are his teachings; so splended is his definition of the duties that man owes to man. So he declares about righteousness:

It is not righteousness that you turn your faces in prayer towards the East or the West; but righteousness is of him who believeth in God and the Last Day and the Angels, and the Scriptures, and the Prophets; who giveth money for God's sake unto his kindred, and unto orphans, and the needy, and the stranger, and those who ask, and for redemption of captives; who is constant at prayer, and giveth alms; and of those who perform their covenant when they have covenanted, and who behave themselves patiently in adversity, and in hardships, and in time of violence.

Muhammad the Prophet was an unlearned man, as the world counts learning. Over and over again he calls himself the "illiterate Prophet," and his followers regard *Al Quran* as a standing miracle, vindicating his claim as a divine Messenger, since it is written in the most perfect Arabic. Yet, unlearned himself, he places learning in the first rank of the things to be desired; he says:

Acquire knowledge; for he who acquires it in the way of the Lord performs an act of piety; who speaks of knowledge, praises God; who seeks it adores God; who dispenses instruction in it bestows alms; and who imparts it to its fitting objects performs an act of devotion to God. Knowledge enables its possessor to distinguish what is forbidden from what is not; it lights the way to heaven; it is our friend in the desert, our society in solitude, our companion when bereft of friends; it guides us to happiness; it sustains us in misery; it is our ornament in the company of friends; it serves as an armour against our enemies. With knowledge, the servant of God rises to the height of goodness and to a noble position, associates with sovereigns in this world, and attains to the perfection of happiness in the next.

So again, with a just discrimination of values, this Teacher, for whom so many died, declares:

The ink of the scholar is more precious than the blood of the martyr.

This sentence should be emblazoned in letters of gold on the wall of every school established by Musalmans, for the children of Islam have ever rushed joyously to martyrdom, but in late centuries—things are rapidly changing now—they have honoured scholars but little.

33

3

Ali, the beloved son-in-law of the Prophet, gave a noble definition of science:

The essence of science is the enlightenment of the heart; truth is its principal object; inspiration its guide; reason its acceptor; God its inspirer; the words of man its utterer.

It was these lofty views of the value of learning which led to the philosophy of the Saracens, the science of the Moors. When it is charged against Islam that it is not progressive, that its peoples lag behind other nations in the value set on learning and on science, its assailants, unless they ignore history, should surely seek for some reason than the religion itself to account for the stagnation of the latter days. For it was Ali, building on the foundation laid by the Prophet himself, who began the definite teaching which, after a hundred years of quiet growth in Arabia, burst upon Europe as a splendid light and, brought by the Moors to Spain, made possible the rebirth of learning in Christendom. It was Islam which, in Arabia and Egypt, in the colleges of Baghdad and Cairo, took up the Neoplatonic heritage, despised and rejected by Christendom as " pagan", after the slaying of Hypatia, and saved its priceless riches to hand them on for European use. It was the value set on knowledge, in obedience to the Prophet's teaching, which led one branch of his followers to devote themselves to study in Arabia, while the other set out to the East and the West with the conquering sword which made Islam's mighty Empire. The students laboured unweariedly in philosophy and science while the warriors hewed their way to power, so that behind

the victorious sword there ever
followed the lamp of knowledge.
Philosophy and science trod in the
foot-prints left by the conqueror.
First along the north of Africa the
hosts of Islam fought their way
and planted their banner; then
from Africa into Spain, to found
there the Moorish Empire. Uni-
versities arose, and students flocked
to them from all parts of Europe,
for in Christendom science was un-
known, astronomy and mathematics had vanished, chemistry
had not risen from its Egyptian
tomb. Knowledge was brought

by the conquering Moors, and Pope Sylvester II in his youth, was a student in the University of Cordova, learning the elements of geometry and mathematics, which aroused later the horror of his ignorant priesthood. I have summed up elsewhere, in speaking on this subject, something of the science brought into Europe by the Moors:

They take up mathematics from the Hindu and the Greek; they discover equations of the second degree; then the quadratic; then the binomial theorem; they discover the sine and cosine in

trigonometry; they make the first tele-
scope: they study the stars; they measure
the size of the earth; they make a new
architecture; they discover a new music;
they teach scientific agriculture; they
bring manufactures to the highest pitch of
excellence.

Nor was all this brought to
Europe only. India knows the
splendid architecture of the
Mughals, of whom it was justly
said:

They built like giants, and finished
like jewellers.

Some of the most wonderful
architectural triumphs of India are
the work of the Musalmans, and

India has been enriched by these treasures, poured into her lap by her Muhammadan children. Their influence may be traced also in Hindu architecture, for no art can be imprisoned within the limits of a creed or a race.

It is an interesting side-issue that much of the incurable suspicion with which official Christianity has regarded science is due to the fact that science returned to Europe under the banner of the Arabian Prophet, and was therefore regarded as a heresy; science to the orthodox was anti-Christian, and they looked on it with hatred and with horror; anyone who cares to read the epithets hurled by the Christians against the Prophet of Islam will understand that anything brought to Christendom in his name would inevitably fall under the ban of the Church. During these early centuries of the life of Islam, the truths of science were spoken out at the risk of life, limb and liberty; the cruel expulsion of the Moors from Spain ended the long struggle and was one of the causes of the downfall of Spain from her place of pride. During

these centuries also there were born
to Islam some of the acutest meta-
physicians and the profoundest
philosophers that the world has
known. They revived and car-
ried further in Europe the philosophy which was the life of Greece,
and is the Vedanta of the Hindu.
In the writings of the great Doctors
of Islam, the same splendid metaphysic is found which is the glory
of the Vedanta, and here lies one of
the reasons for union between
Hindus and Musalmans in modern
India. Islam and Hinduism can
meet each other, and clasp hands

in brotherly friendship on this high
ground of philosophy and metaphysic, common to both, Musalman Doctors and Hindu Acharyas
standing side by side. And here
may I say a word of gentle reproach
to my brothers of Islam?—" This
metaphysic is yours, but it is of
value for the world; why do you
not translate it for the benefit of
India and of the West?" When I
wanted to study it, I found it in
Arabic, or in the monkish Latin
of the Middle Ages; finally I dis-
covered some fragmentary translations in French—the French

apparently valuing these treasures of Islam more than their legitimate owners—and found myself on familiar ground, so close was their philosophy to that of the Hindus. By the translation of these works a point of union, then, would be found between Musalmans and Hindus, and they would find themselves at one in philosophy and metaphysic while differing in rites. And, secondly, such translations would vindicate Islam in the eyes of the world, as translations of the Acharyas have vindicated Hinduism. Europe will recognise and honour the Muhammadan learning of the East, and we shall hear no more of the reproach that Islam favours ignorance.

Let us consider next the attitude of Islam towards women. One of the commonest sneers at Islam in the West is that it teaches that women have no souls. This is most certainly false: *Al Quran* says:

Whoso doeth evil shall be rewarded for it, and shall not find any patron or helper beside God; but whoso doeth good works, whether he be male or female, and is a true believer, they shall be admitted into paradise and shall not in the least be unjustly dealt with . . . True believers of either sex, and the devout men and the devout women, and the men of veracity and the women of veracity, and the patient men and the patient women, and the humble men and the humble women, and the almsgivers of either sex, and the men who fast and the women who fast, and the chaste men and the chaste women, and those of either sex who remember God frequently; for them hath God prepared forgiveness and a great reward. . . . I will not suffer the work of him among you who worketh to be lost, whether he be male or female. The one of you is from the other.

Men and women are thus put on a perfectly equal footing in matters of religion.

But, it is said, Islam allows polygamy. That is so. But in justice to Islam two facts should be considered: first, the historical. The people for whose uplifting Islam was given were living, to a very large extent, in promiscuity; sex morality had no existence among them; to command them to observe monogamy would have been useless; only gradual reform was possible. Hence the Prophet, being wise and far-seeing, first laid down, as a limitation of promiscuity, that a man might have four wives only; then, gradually to

47

eliminate polygamy, that a hus-
band might only take a second wife
if he could treat her in all respects
as the first. His teaching is working
towards the result aimed at, and
educated Musalmans—at least in
India, of other lands I cannot speak
—are rising out of polygamy.

The second fact is the present
relation between men and women
in all " civilised " countries. The
true and righteous sex-relation between one man and one woman is
preached as an ideal in some countries, but is generally practised in
none. Islam permits polygamy;

Christendom forbids but winks at it, provided that no *legal* tie exists with more than one. There is pretended monogamy in the West, but there is really polygamy without responsibility; the " mistress " is cast off when the man is weary of her, and sinks gradually to be the " woman of the streets ", for the first lover has no responsibility for her future, and she is a hundred times worse off than the sheltered wife and mother in the polygamous home. When we see the thousands of miserable women who crowd the streets of western towns during the night, we must surely feel that it does not lie in western mouth to reproach Islam for its polygamy. It is better for a woman, happier for a woman, more respectable for a woman, to live in Muhammadan polygamy, united to one man only, with the legitimate child in her arms, and surrounded with respect, than to be seduced, cast out into the streets—perhaps with an illegitimate child outside the pale of law—unsheltered and uncared for, to become the victim of any passer-by, night after night, rendered incapable of motherhood, despised

of all. It is good for Society
that monogamy should be held up
as an ideal, for its public recogni-
tion as right, and the inner shame
connected with resort to prostitu-
tion are purifying forces; but monogamy is not practised where there
is one legal wife and hidden non-
legalised sexual relations. The
recognised polygamy of the East
degrades the social conscience
more than the unrecognised polygamy of the West—" hypocrisy is
a homage vice pays to virtue "
—but the happiness and dig-
nity of the woman suffer less

under the first than under the second.

Apart from this, Musalman women have been far better treated than western women by the law. Until lately English law, for instance, confiscated the married woman's property as though marriage were a felony, forfeited her earnings, gave her no claim to her own children. By the laws of Islam her property was carefully guarded. And it is noteworthy how great a part women have played in Muslim countries as rulers, and in statesmanship.

" But Islam is a persecuting faith, a religion of the sword." Alas! most faiths must confess to persecution and bloodshed. The followers of Islam have wrested the teachings of their Prophet as other faiths have done, and there are no teachings of persecution in *Al Quran* so cruel as those in the *Old Testament*, still declared by Christian Churches to be the "Word of God", though no longer obeyed. The Prophet Muhammad constantly declares that there is but one religion, Islam. But Islam in his mouth only means surrender to the

53

Divine Will, and he calls all
holy men of old, men who lived
long before his time, followers of
Islam. Surrender to the Divine Will
is recognised by every religionist as
a duty, and Islam *as used by the Prophet*, has this inclusive meaning; in
this sense every true faith is Islam,
and every one who surrenders his
will to God is a true follower of
Islam.   Once more listen to *Al
Quran*:

There is no distinction between
Prophets . . . Every one of the Prophets
believed in God, His angels and His
scriptures and His apostles. We make

no distinction at all between His apostles
. . . Say, we believe in God and that
which hath been sent down unto us, and
that which was sent down unto Abraham
and Ismail and Isaac and Jacob and
other tribes, and that which was delivered
to Moses and Jesus and the Prophets
from their Lord; we make no distinction
between any of them . . . They who
believed in God and His apostles and
make no distinction between any of them,
unto those will we give their reward, and
God is gracious and merciful.

It is true that he commanded:
" Slay the infidels." But he
defines the infidels as those who do
not follow righteousness. There
are two sets of these commands:

" Slay the infidels "; and: " Slay the infidel when he attacks you, and will not let you practise your religion." It has been authoritatively ruled by Muhammadan jurists that when there is an absolute and a conditioned command, the latter must be taken as defining and limiting the former. Moreover the Prophet lays down with regard to infidels:

If they desist from opposing thee, what is already past shall be forgiven them.

And he says:

Invite men unto the way of the Lord by wisdom and mild exhortation; and dispute with them in the most condescending manner, for the Lord well knoweth him who strayeth from His path, and He well knoweth those who are rightly directed. Let there be no violence in religion. If they embrace Islam they are surely directed; but if they turn their backs, verily unto thee belongeth preaching only.

Nor should it be forgotten that some of the exhortations, now interpreted as universal, were really addressed by the Prophet, as a general, to troops just going into battle, often against overwhelming

57

odds, and were intended to rouse them to courage in the impending fight. His practice may be taken, surely, as a commentary on his precepts; and we find that he stopped the universal practice of killing prisoners taken in battle, and taught his soldiers to treat their captured foes with the utmost kindness.

Futher, we read that even controversy was not to be harsh and bitter.

Revile not the idols which they invoke beside God, lest they maliciously revile God without knowledge. . . .

Unto every one of you have we given a law and an open path; and if God had pleased He had surely made you one people. But He hath thought fit to give you different laws, that He might try you in that which He hath given you respectively. Therefore strive to excel each other in good works; unto God shall ye all return, and then will He declare unto you that concerning which ye have disagreed.

In speaking thus I have had a purpose beyond that of amusing you for an hour, by repeating things that many of you must know as well as, or better than, I. And that purpose is the drawing together of Musalmans and

Hindus, for India can never become a nation until Hindus, Zoroastrians, Christians and Musalmans understand each other. Shall we not all put aside theological hatreds and feel as brothers? Shall not the Musalman cease to mutter " Giaour ", and the Hindu cease to whisper " Mlechchha ", and the Christian cease to say " Heathen "? Shall we not learn to respect each other's faith, and reverence each other's worship? There is no need for conversion from one religion to another; each is a Ray of the Sun of Truth. We

Theosophy and
The Theosophical Society

The Theosophical Society, founded in 1875, is a worldwide body whose primary object is Universal Brotherhood based on the realization that life, in all its diverse forms, human and non-human, is indivisibly One. The Society imposes no belief on its members, who are united by a common search for truth and the desire to learn the meaning and purpose of existence by engaging themselves in study, reflection, purity of life and loving service.

Theosophy is the wisdom underlying all religions when they are stripped of accretions and superstitions. It offers a philosophy which renders life intelligible and demonstrates that justice and love guide the cosmos. Its teachings aid the unfoldment of the latent spiritual nature in the human being, without dependence or fear.

For general information, please contact:

International Secretary
The Theosophical Society
Adyar, Chennai 600 020, India
Fax: (91-44) 490-2706 Tel: 491-2474
e-mail: intl.hq@ts-adyar.org
website:http://www.ts-adyar.org

For catalogue, enquiries and orders of books and magazines, contact:

The Theosophical Publishing House
Adyar, Chennai 600 020, India
Fax: (91-44) 490-1399
Tel: 491-1338 & 446-6613
e-mail: tphindia@md5.vsnl.net.in
        theos.soc@gems.vsnl.net.in